# Celebrating Moon Festival

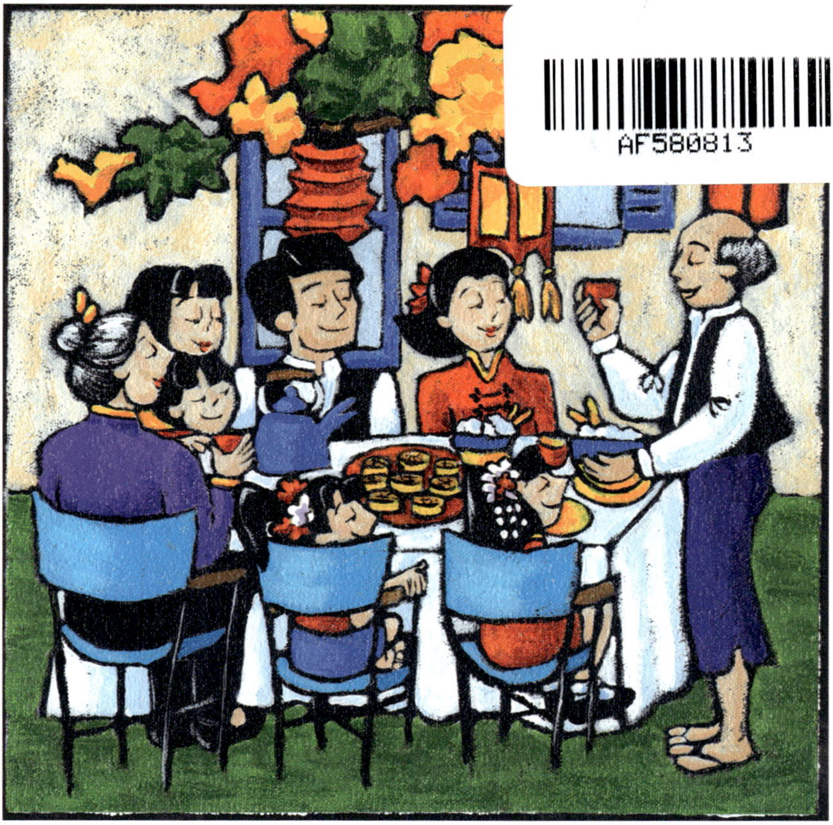

by Gloria Rose    illustrated by Janet Nelson

Scott Foresman
is an imprint of

PEARSON

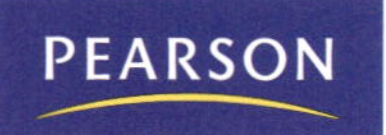

Glenview, Illinois • Boston, Massachusetts • Mesa, Arizona
Shoreview, Minnesota • Upper Saddle River, New Jersey

Every effort has been made to secure permission and provide appropriate credit for photographic material. The publisher deeply regrets any omission and pledges to correct errors called to its attention in subsequent editions.

Unless otherwise acknowledged, all photographs are the property of Pearson.

Photo locations denoted as follows: Top (T), Center (C), Bottom (B), Left (L), Right (R), Background (Bkgd)

Illustrations by Janet Nelson

8 ©Jim Richardson/CORBIS

ISBN 13: 978-0-328-39329-9
ISBN 10: 0-328-39329-0



1 2 3 4 5 6 7 8 9 10 V010 17 16 15 14 13 12 11 10 09 08

It was the day of the Moon Festival. Mai's whole family was coming for dinner.

"Did you get moon cakes?" Mai asked.

"I want moon cakes," cried Mai.

"We have eight moon cakes," said Mother. "But it's wrong to touch them now. We must make dinner first."

"We'll tie lights above us like more moons," said Mother. "We will say thank you for all we have."

"I will say thank you for moon cakes," thought Mai.

The family ate dinner together. Grandfather told the story about a lady who lived in the moon.

"We can each make a wish," he said.

Mai looked at the moon cakes.

She made the same wish she had made all day. Then she gave a happy laugh. She knew her wish would soon come true!

# Moon Cakes and the Moon Festival

The Chinese Moon Festival is a little like Thanksgiving. It is celebrated at the end of the harvest season. On this day, Chinese families gather together. They tell the story about a lady who lived in the moon. They give each other small, round moon cakes. Some moon cakes have a yellow egg yolk in the middle. The yolk looks like a bright, full moon!